J'Parlé

Live•Love•Speak•Create

Poetry Anthology

JERICA D. WORTHAM

Copyright © 2018 Jerica D. Wortham

All rights reserved.

ISBN-13: 978-0-9990310-2-5

DEDICATION

This book is dedicated to every artist that has ever been hungry for more; and in that desire for more set out their intention, and made every one of their dreams come true.

CONTENTS

Acknowledgments — i

1. **Imperfect Perfectionist** — 3
Candy Weeks

2. **Thoughts On Beauty** — 7
Tosha Craft

3. **Scribbles** — 21
Webster L. Wortham

4. **Self- Actualization** — 25
Karmen S. Williams

5. **Seasons** — 33
Kenya Turner Washington

6. **My Thoughts Your Fantasy** — 39
Connie Turner

7. **Poetry Of A Lifetime: One Rhyme At A Time** — 45
Demeatrice Hall

8. **Dedication** — 49
Jerica D. Wortham

9. **WOAK** — 55
King Landon

10. **Love In All Its Madness** — 63
Bri Gambino

11. **Musing** — 69
Marissa Fraser

12. **Pieces To The Puzzle** — 77
Charnica Jordachea

13. **A New Concept For A Beginning Man** — 85
Kenneth Sanders III

ACKNOWLEDGMENTS

I would like to take a moment to thank every author for their contribution to this anthology. I am so proud of each and every one of them for taking a chance on themselves and being vulnerable with you the readers.

To Finally Focus Photography. Thank you for always coming through in the clutch. Your professionalism is epically dope!

Last but not least to my husband Webster, and my children Solomon and Jonah thank you for sharing your time while we worked to make dreams come true. Love you all like air.

J Parle' Publishing Poetry Anthology

1
IMPERFECT
PERFECTIONIST
CANDY
WEEKS

Lukewarm

I feel pulled
To one side more than the other
Straddling the fence
One foot in Hell
The other in Heaven
One foot in Heaven
The other in the grave
Each keeping me from the other totally
I feel grey
 Heaven telling me I've had enough Hell
And
Hell telling me I can't live in between

I hope I make up my mind…
Cj 2/13/11

Reevaluation

Trying to hold it all together
Atlas…. Drop it
What I'd like to do VS. life
No, I know how it may sound
Just looking for a way around

Keeping my eyes open
No more entrapment
A.K.A. love filled abusive relationship
That takes me for all I have
Silver and gold, I have none
I need some
time to explore my mind
Who am I…
Do I like who I am?
Is that based upon who likes me?
Where's my joy…

Cj

I lied

He asked if I still write, didn't know he cared or liked.
I said "NO", but I do.
I keep my writings in my head.
Beautiful poems; too
tired to grab pen or pad.
Aggravated, distracted really by the enemy I once called My Angel.

I write,
I write every night
The song in my head that plays on my heart.
There is a love in my life
Though we're apart.
Our spirits speak, Our dreams reach, Our souls connect.
Mind, Body and Spirit we know each other most; we Love each other best!

Cj 8/6/08

2

THOUGHTS ON BEAUTY
TOSHA CRAFT

Beautiful Things

Beautiful things

Never stay beautiful

For long

Like days turn into nights

Age takes over

And time

Causes things to

Shift and change

Beauty fades

Roses wilt

Women age

Boobs sag

Milk spoils

All becoming

Reflections

Of their former

Selves

And to the beholder

These become

Less useful

Less appealing

Than they once were

To the untrained eye

Yes

Beauty fades

Time and age

Take over

Things begin

To shift and change

Metamorphosis begins

And growth replaces

The former things

Roses die to themselves

Become paper thin

And black

Only to be reborn

With the change

Of the season

Birthing new buds

In spring

Women too

Once so young

And supple

Breast held high

Begin to droop

With age

Backs bend and stoop

To morph into

Silver-haired

Wisdom bearers

And milk sours

Becoming bitter and tart

Losing its savor in

The curdled taste

And putrid smell

Yet

When added to batter

Can produce a cake

Sweet and moist

Full of flavor

No beautiful things

Never stay beautiful

For long

They shift and change

Morph and grow

Into other

Forms of beauty

Things I Needed to Hear

She never told me I was beautiful

And isn't that what every little girl

Wishes for

To be the apple of her mother's eye

So I searched for love and approval

While anticipated hugs were traded

For poisonous lashes and

The harsh lash of her tongue

A trait picked up from her father

She didn't quite know how to love

Took me years to fully comprehend

That acidic fruits can cause craters

And any dentist will tell you that

Cavities can only be filled – but

The damage is permanent

All I wanted was for her to sing me

Lullabies

Hold me like I was bone of her bone

Flesh of her flesh

It is because of this neglect that

I too know why the caged bird sings

And yet there are some things

More painful than lack of words

He

Came into my life when I was

A 13-year-old girl with less

Self-esteem than breast

Contrary to popular belief

Blended families mean nothing

If there are no boundaries established

My lack of exposure had not

Prepared me for a 16-year old pedophile

In training

Late nights he would hold my hand

Tell me I was beautiful

Feed my soul with syrupy sweet lies

The flavor of Now & Laters

Convinced me that he loved me

And who was I to argue

Had I ever known love

In my experience it seemed

Innocent enough at first

Until the night he kissed me

I'm not sure if I liked it – but

I enjoyed the sturdiness of his fingers

As he held my naïve and easy led hand

Hand-holding turned into hands in his

Pants

Sweet kisses became the acrid taste

Of precum on my tongue

And I knew it was wrong

Had never been with a boy unless

You count that time at summer camp

When I let that boy grind on me or

That time in the laundry room

A neighbor and I were dared

To show each other our parts

We tried to fit piece A into Slot B

But could never figure out the logistics

Decided to tell everyone we did it –

Kiddie games

But this – this was no game

And he would not be satisfied

With only street cred

Isn't it ironic that one's innocence

Can be completely shattered with the

Perforation of a tiny little hymen

For two years I gave him my time

Let him play with my body

While he fucked with my mind

And no one ever bothered to notice

Why I failed to smile – Why I was considered

A moody and over-sensitive child

I had heard from the girls in the

Neighborhood

That the first time was supposed to be

Memorable

I have spent a lifetime trying to

Forget

No

She never told me I was beautiful

But at times like these

I wish she had

Epiphany of Me

I worked out every day

Never put anything but salad

On my plate

And still gained six pounds

Went round after round

With the misperception

Self-misdirection

That I was not good enough

These jeans didn't fit me

Cute enough

And I had the blues

Laced up my shoes to run

Another mile

While hiding my discontent

Behind a fake ass smile

The truth is:

This struggle to achieve

What the world says

I should be

Is exhausting

This course I am on

Is emotionally costing

And I have

Nothing else to give

You see

I was too busy

Trying to live the mirage

Of the constant barrage

The media tries to

Force-feed down my throat

Got chocked up

Every time I realized

That I may never again

See another size 5

Until one day

I heard a man say

That true beauty

Had to lie

Within the recesses

Of my own two eyes

One simple statement

Sparked a change in me

My viewpoint shifted

From this epiphany

And I began to clearly see

That these big hips

And thick thighs

Are prize possessions

An open confession

That I am a queen

This ample bottom

A grown man's dream

And every curve and dimple

Is just a simple

Part of me

But they have never defined

What I am

Or

What I should be

3
SCRIBBLES

WEBSTER L. WORTHAM

February 13, 2018

It's Midnight and I'm restless, Listening to trains cross
Must be a thousand cars, one for each of racing thoughts
Now I hear sirens... I wonder what just happened?
was it related to the train, you know coincidences happens
I'm spazzin, it's prolly from the lack of napping, and that 3am tapping on
        my do'(or) won't keep me happy
I'm guessing, That siren wasn't for the train,
Maybe it's a mission for cop to help a victim out the pain
Help a mother in a strain, and not another being slain
These people deaf to the ring, or too blind to see you scream
I open windows for my light with no blinds behind the screen
So your eyes can't help but see, the reflection of what is me...

Greatness

June 4, 2016

Head tilted forward

Elongated Neck

Body like a Coke bottle

Taste buds wet.

Crossed over feet

Pushed up pecks

Wife beater covering

Legs show flesh

Hands up high

Couple twists of the wrist

I'm loving it all, and can barely resist.

Either in front of the mirror

Or a quick stop in the hall

Whether you ready to serve, or ready to ball

The act is pure sexy from beginning to end

I like you fresh out the shower, with a tooted tail end

Crisp edges for business

Loose ends for fun

It's something about watching a woman put her hair in a bun!

April 19, 2017

Every scribble a deposit to help decrease my family debt
Ice cold with the words, bet I can make an alpha bet
David with these letters man, heart to kill a giant
The strength is in the hair
Solomon mane look like a lions
Solomon is my son if you ain't get that last line
Trying to teach em about this game.........
National past time
Every try ain't a homer
Sometimes you pop fly
Stay in place when you on base, and at times it's better to slide
Keep your eye on the ball, and swing when there's no doubt
By his stripes you are healed, so 3 strikes is not out

Second scribble has no riddle just a little more of the same
16 was mad rough, in December that all changed
Felt like I was under water had to swallow with every fail
But when Jonah came through its like I swam right out that whale
Jonah is my son
My third blessing to shield
Can't wait to teach him how to move on this crooked playing field.
Every "hut" ain't a first down
Sometimes you gotta average 4
And when you try to tackle life, make sure you always stay low
Make sure you stay solid, look em straight in the eye
Stay fly, keep God first, and promise to always try.

-Love Pops

4

SELF-ACTUALIZATION

KARMEN S. WILLIAMS

Love So Real

I thought I was in love with this man right
But it turns out it was an aim to be lead contrite
To the ways of which I was taught
And brought up
From Saturday to Sunday
From every day in June to May

Yea, I knew better
I've even seen stormy weather
Which was mostly likely my fault
In the arms of the wrong I sought
A place that I could call home
Cause home is where the heart is, right
Such love beyond the use of sight
Or so I thought

Instead of a place to lay my head
I received an area that I made my bed
And then had to lie in
Filled with sin since day one
It's like running away with no place to run
I went searching and searching
Not realizing that the answer was right here
A love so real

Immediately I fell to my knees that are raw as ever
Worldly ties I began to sever
When I realized that love could not be purchased
Not with earthly material things it's worthless
To the God who created me with purpose and a plan
Submerged with love and all power in His hand
Where I fall weak, He makes me strong
Where I fall short, He forgives all wrong
See He's more than life to me
He is my air that I'm allowed to breathe
He is my peace in the middle of the storm

He is my fire that keeps me warm

He's my all and all
Who loves me enough to call
Me His friend
When I turned on Him at the likes of men
He forgives beyond belief
He restores with the greatest relief
That balm in Gilead one said
Who heals from the crown of my head
Down to the ground I tread

Now that's love
No greater could be found
Trust I searched all around
All along He was right there
Full of hope and love to share
Why didn't I notice before
He was all I needed, nothing more
I immediately gave my life to this love
He is a love so real…

I've never known love, love, love, a love like this before
Cause love was never love
Until he came down from above
And took my place
Removed my disgrace
That was set upon my head from my wrong doings

I can't understand how someone like Him
Can love someone like me
And die on the cross
That I might be free
From death
And the penalty of sin
And completely accepted me in
To His family, heir to His throne
Now I know how it feels to belong

That is love
It's a love so real
So easy to feel
Cause he paid my price
Automatically made me right
No more searching and searching
Cause Eureka I've found
Better than gold
This love cannot be sold
Out or in for nothing, zilch, nada
Greatest love from my heavenly father
He is a love so real…

Failed Nation
Karmen S. Williams, Dock Williams III, Brian S. Williams

For many centuries there's been pressing memories
And phantom pains of locks and chains
On the hands, feet and mind of the people
Because of foolish thoughts of oppression
And compression of a people
Into tiny rooms and spaces
Invading the places that the people call home

Homelands ravaged
And savaged by creatures
That call themselves civilized
And they didn't realize
Or didn't care that stealing anything
Is against God
I mean how can you rob
A land of its people
And justify within that they're not equal
Or even human
And I'm assuming
No one had a conscious

Years later when someone finally gets some sense
And decide to free the people of some of the tense
And strains of slavery
There still is a lock on the minds
Reversing time to continue in ways
Of prejudice and bias
Once again in a land
Where they ain't paid no rent

The idea that dark skin is a threat to be feared and neutralized
Ingrained in the hearts and mind of this very nation and futurized
Shed tears for my brothers who wear the uniform of this land

Unable to stand tall without a door locked or purse clutch in their hands
Were the tours in war zones not enough for you to realize
We are the same, yet no respect just terrorized
I too should be free to wave my American flag with the same pride
Ancestors built this great nation only receiving blood, sweat, and tears
    as payment
Constantly asked to stop bringing up slavery
But it is not us who insist on providing a daily reminder
This was a county built by us but not for us

Unable to take a knee for the country to acknowledge the racism
Increased waves of confederate flags speaking of heritage
How can you wave a defeated flag and still profit
While we the people suffer either way
But we the people don't need your stingy reparations
We demand your respect
And restructuring of these institutional oppressions

We the people need to work hard
At remembering who we are
And the scars that make us strong
We come from a long, long history
Of mysteries of survival and we will continue

We the people we need to refuse to live up to the stereotypes
Reach for new excellence not built on this failed nation's standards
Stop the modern day mandingo fights, traded for guns and knives
Ethnic suicide, self-genocide, we are perpetuating the wishes of others
Gangs built as shields to protect the community from the violence and
    brutality
Perverted and minimalized to territory, colors towards degradation of
    that same community

We the people need to keep the hope
We the people need to keep the faith
And we the people need to keep a REVOLUTION

Beautiful Black Skin

I had nothing to do with this beautiful black skin
I find myself wrapped in
But I have something to do with how I treat people
Regardless of the hate they give
The lies they live
I have the power to be me
Beyond adversities and others' realities
I live my own bold statement daily
By the love I wear on my face and give with whole self
I stand against stereotypes of black = violence, black = evil, black = bad
Well I take that back because I'm bad and I know it
Like the kings and queens I descended from
As the lands of prosperity I uprooted come
Back to my mind every time
I step out in this beautiful black skin

5 SEASONS
KENYA TURNER WASHINGTON

Bottled Tears

Taking all my tears, all my fears and placing them in a bottle on the shelf.
Not throwing them away,
But keeping them close
Because I may need them for another day.
Need them as a reminder of my trials and tribulations
And the strength that got me to this day.
I need you to remember that scars are just a reminder that you made it another day.
And you are here to tell your story.

2018 is my year of YES
    Yes, I will love myself
    Yes, I will follow my dreams
        Walk away from negative people
    Yes, I will start my own businesses
    Travel more, protect my energy
Yes, I'm bottling those tears placing them on the shelf.
Walking in my truth and loving on myself.
Loving all of me.
    Loving every dimple, curve, and each loc of my fabulous hair.
    These long nails, and all the dark chocolate that drips from myself.

Every inappropriate touch, every fear, every lie that was spoken, for my childhood that was snatched.
    Yes, I'm bottling those tears and putting them on a shelf.
    Yes, I will play too much.
    I will dance every chance I get.
    Trust again
    And allow my husband to love all of me
    Kenya now and the Kenya I'm destined to be.

Bottled Tears

I Am that I Am

Most of you have forgotten who I am
Most of you put your complete trust in man
Husband, woman, pastor, doctor, momma, daddy and so called friends
With all that being said, for the life of you, you can't understand
Understand why life keeps happening over and over again
Bills they coming
Sickness you accepting it
Lies you keep believing them
I Am light in the darkness
Income were there is none
Strength for the weakest
I Am the truth that you seek, there is none like me
I Am guidance to the lost sheep
You are searching for truth, trust there is none like me
That abusive relationship that you refused to leave
I gave you a way out and you still didn't thank me
I Am food on the table, a meal when there was none
Healer of your heart, mind, body and soul
When the doctors gave up, I stepped right in
No thanks no acknowledgement but I still healed
I Am that I Am
I fought the case in the courtroom
You should have got life, but I got you ten
I heard every cry
I caught every tear, all those fears
I opened doors that nobody can shut
I Am called many names but few really know
Stop taking me for granted
I stand here patiently waiting
I Am That I Am

Queen I Am

It's okay to be your own hero. It's okay to encourage yourself.
It's okay to say dang girl you did that
Dang girl you does this.
Some of you are raising children alone
Healing your own bodies...
Yes we do that
Going to school, being a wife and mother.
Baby you are the hero of your story.

I'm something like a hero, brave, warrior with the heart of a lion
Light maker, way maker, risk taker
With the strength of my ancestors standing by me
Yes, I do all that

    Queen I am
I looked death in the eye and still managed to survive.

    Queen I am
Was given a death sentence at the age of 13 crippled in a wheelchair was
        the future that was spoken over me.

    Queen I am
But I'm here still standing on my own two feet with my head held high.
There has been tears and heartache but I'm a hero, so I still survive.

    Queen I am
I'm my own hero how you say I've had a stroke, heart condition, Lupus,
        RA, and now they want to test me for another rear disease.

Queen I am
Plus, they said I would never have kids because I was barren
But here I stand with not 1 but 2 beautiful children who have been
        Prophesied to go speak to the nations.
Never giving up because there is so much more to see.
So many more chapters to my magnificent story.

    Queen   Yes   I   Am!!!

6

MY THOUGHTS
YOUR FANTASY

CONNIE TURNER

Lust!

Lustful, silky thoughts of you

Your beautiful rippled skin touching me

Hands that can't seem to get enough

My lips, my hips, my soul are yours to mold

       These are...Lustful thoughts of you

My body tingles at the very thought of us

Hard muscles that touch my softness

I caress you, and kiss your skin

And ask, where do I begin

       These are...Lustful thoughts of you

Chest, arms and thighs

Oh my god... I am so high,

The creaminess of our juices, the scent of us

The taste of me on your lips

       These are...Lustful thoughts of you

Breathing hard, dripping with sweat

Still you want me... you lust is not spent

You touch me and kiss my spot

Oh damn... now I'm so hot

Can't let you go, no not now

Explosive, fiery, magnificent, powerful

Satisfied for the moment, wow

Holding me so soft in your strong arms

Yes, lust now sated

      These are...Lustful thoughts of you

♥Connie©

Naughty

I'm gonna lay here and let you look

Are you wondering if I will touch myself or play out scenes from a book

My clit throbs yearning for your fingers

It pulses with need and begs you to linger

Let me whisper naughty thoughts in your ear

Tell you where I want you~ front or rear

I don't need to ask if you're hard for me

Your body betrays you and shows its need

My nipples are hard~ my walls are wet

Should I let you release this pent up frustration… no not yet!

Your tongue is fantastic as you show me your skills

It teases me all over and promises me thrills

A few shots of Tequila and a suck of lime

You can make me cum multiple times

Do you want me in a negligee, or butt naked

Just be damn good so I won't have to fake it!!

I like it naughty…and sometimes rough…

You know baby… not that same ole stuff

♥Connie

Foreplay n' then some

Your voice caresses me like hot oil

It's smooth and deep and speaks through lips that caress my very soul

You say words that my ears need to hear and my heart already knows

Lips placed so sensuously on my thighs

Like feathers from the birds that fly so high

Placing light kisses on the back of my knees

Baby please don't make me plead

With hands that tease me you take me there

I want to touch, but you say... stay here

Experience it, feel it, give in to it, love it

Eyes closed now, I see the place we share

My turn baby!

I whisper in your ear the words of a wanton woman

Explicit, enthralling, meant only for you to hear

I love your skin, you smell so damn good

I'm going to touch you and tease you

Lick you and please you

My lips now on your body

Blowing kisses everywhere, my tongue touches and juices start to flow

Wait! I want to take this slow…

Baby oil smoothes the way as I massage your soul

Can you feel the love and yearning that flows through my fingers?

It's electrifying, nerves that now tingle

My nails circle your nipples and navel

Oh yea sexy, now you're able!

Our turn!

Our bodies are like the earth's rotation, so flawless in its movement

So perfect in its rhythm, slow and deliberate

Stimulating the core of me, awake now with the promise of fire

So sure of what's to come and calm this burning desire

So hot, so wet, so good words spoken through the moans

I respond… oh yea daddy take me home!

♥Connie©

June 3rd 2011

7

POETRY OF A LIFETIME: ONE RHYME AT A TIME

DEMEATRICE HALL

Mother 🌼

A Mother is to me all that a woman should be.

A Mother is to me; in a few words, Specialty, Royalty, Humility, & Honesty.

A Mother is to me L-O-V-E.
A Mother is to me a gift from above.

A Mother is in one word "Everything"
For you see without Mother there would be no me.

A Mother sacrifices herself for her child: Even when we choose to run wild.

A Mother is a blessing; you may not always show her that you care; But a Mother will always be there.

A Mother is a lesson in life. For some the word Mother also means wife.

A Mother is the flower blooming in the spring. A Mother is a song to sing.

A Mother is what God gave as one more example of Grace, Favor, and Love.

A Mother is all that and more, and today Mother I want you to know it is you whom I Love, Cherish & Adore!

My Time

I feel that my time has finally come. No longer shall I be shun.

I will write for the world to see just how beautiful poetry can be.

I've written for years. Happy, Sad, depressed and tears.

Today I say goodbye to the old fears.

I will choose my words wisely as if I were painting a brightly colored picture for all to see.

As if it were a commercial to advertise me. To sum it all it's just Poetry.

My canvas is the notepad in which I write.

The paint is the words that I recite.

The beauty of the art is keeping it tight.

Keeping those things in mind.
It must be right.

Again, I say this is my time!

Melody

Some notes are sang high while others are sung low.

The melody is you and I.
We don't always agree yet we keep the melody.

The beat may change , but the love remains the same.

Like the chirp of a bird in a tree.
You are my melody.

The thump of my song; The right of my wrong.

The reason why I press on.
The melody of my song.

8

DEDICATION

JERICA D. WORTHAM

Tribute to Terence Crutcher

Here I am walking around thinking my black is beautiful.
That my tone and stature were acquiescent to nostalgia sure to come of time and places
Time and places I was considered
Regal
Worthy
I was loved.
Here I am thinking my tone and stature served as reminders of strength and security.
Teddy bear hugs
And midnight skies
I was the protector.
How did that go unnoticed?
How did that get tarnished?
How was I ever considered a big bad dude?

Here I am thinking my hands
Gentle, firm, and strong
Signals of love and peace
Pressed together during hymnals
Beckoning praise while singing songs
Musically inclined
Hands raised frequently to the heavens in worship
Raised frequently in thanksgiving
Hands raised frequently in service
Now placed in the air gave sign of submission.
Beckoning. humanity.
Reminding you that my life matters
Take notice
I am here
How did those hands....
Those hands get tarnished?
How was I ever considered non compliment?

Here I am thinking I had the right to the inalienable right of LIFE
Life, liberty, and the pursuit of happiness. How sad that living is now evading us.....
Life so precious taken
With no consequence
Here I am believing in justice for all
But somehow my justice didn't count
Here I am
A reminder that the remnants that have plagued this very ground we are standing are still here
That the more things change the more they stay the same
What does it all mean?

Here I am thinking that we can use today as a start of something beautiful.
That the world is watching and waiting
That we should make it worth their while
Here I am thinking
That the tears were not in vain.
That the hurt is serving a purpose.
That even Christ suffered before people truly understood the weight that love can carry
Here I am
heavy in love
Choosing change
Even when I'm unsure of the method
Vacillating between peace and let's mutha down
But always thinking
Always praying
Always choosing
Love

Wife To Wife
Tribute to Melissa Lewis (You are still in my prayers)

I tried to write something fancy
Something worthy of the love that the two of you shared
A highlight reel of a fairytale Romance
Design to set a standard
Ordained by God
From the beginning
But what do you say?
How do you speak to the heart of someone that's seen forever?
How do you fix your lips to say I trust God but I don't like this one bit
It feels icky
Wife to wife
I offer you my solidarity
Whisper prayers through a smushed up face
Finding peace in Him being fluent in tears
It makes the difference
The difference being hope
Hope that even though the future was planned to include this beautiful
    soul it will still be worth seeking
That beauty for ashes is what you will be reaping
For he knows the plans he has for you
And he promised that those that mourn will be comforted too
So even if it feels like your taking Ls through this knight
Just know in the morning you'll be straight like the rook
Find peace that this is the end of the chapter.
Not the end of the book.

Tribute to Hazel Smith-Jones
(Last known Tulsa Race Massacre Survivor in Tulsa)

This is not a fairytale
There is no knight in shining armor
Yet the stories found in between the lines of silenced words
Blocked realities
Unspoken truths
Became their own kind of beautiful
I, with world watching
Shared snapshots of my mental scrapbook
Piecing together fragments of a tapestry that made us
Warmed by memories of a mother's love
A father's devotion
One of 13 finding refuge in fairgrounds
It wasn't fair
But we had each other
Now I, share a tale of loss, and tenacity
A survivor
A testament to the strength of a people
Here I lay
Blessed
A reminder of the hope ingrained in our DNA
99 years of transformation
Seeding possibility in the youth of today
One revelation at a time
One dream at a time
Hoping this one time
History might repeat itself
To that one time
We as a people thrived to the levels we once occupied without a second thought
Meant for greatness
No, this ain't no fairytale
I'm sorry
I have no anecdotes to appease your desire for sensationalism
All I have is me
And all me has is a story of a young girl from Tulsa, Oklahoma that made it through a very precarious situation

It ain't no fairytale
But I
Still...
lived happily ever after.

9
WOAK
WRITINGS OF A KING
KING LANDON

The Good Wife

On the journey to finding myself I found you

You!? More into me than myself had ever seen yet also so much more into me than I currently thought that I would ever be into

In me I found you

Caring enough to recognize the need for me to realize that I am the cause of my own self demise

Loving me more than I then loved myself sometimes, though I cared for and loved everyone else all of the time

Teaching me that indeed I did need everyone's love but to truly be complete I needed to first and most importantly of all love myself

More than my wife you have become the most continuous inspiration I've ever felt

Showing me that in loving myself there is so much more to appreciate about my own life you have simultaneously peaked my motivation

All being said I can only hope to be, have been or one day become the same to you in at least a fraction of a consultation........

I almost fumble the keys as I rush to the car because the doctor said you had fallen into a coma and it wasn't much more that they could do

As she asks "Are we going to see mommy" I unconsciously ignore and put "legnA" in the car because I can't help but think of all the great encouraging and positive things I could have said to you

Hoping that it wasn't me on your mind clouding it with worries and doubts putting your thoughts in a bind wondering with hopes that this is just another argument and like those before we could make it through

Stressing you so much that you saw but acted like you didn't see that light just like you usually do the argument every time we fight and also this time did with our fight thinking that you could make it through it too

I hop in the car now speeding like a demon I race to be by your side because I know you just need my touch

Hating myself because of all the things I said daunted with ridding regret and static

As our little girl yells daddy you forgot my belt and I turn in shock at what she said I panic

I take my eyes off the road and we collide with an "18" wheeler from the incoming traffic

Clutching our baby as we are looking over you as you wake on Saturday as if everything was ok

Like the good wife you are they ask who's the first person you want to see and without missing a beat you said my name

If only I could be there for you instead of missing my opportunity once again

Truth Be Told

More so than often I am beside myself today family, as the present times seem old and new all in one

So do I trust and pick up the false secured laws that never protected us or take my chances with a gun?

As my conscience debates my soul it seems my heart is the judge and my mind is the jury

Though they don't always agree
I refuse to look for an answer or post on social media, my aim isn't attention seeking nor to gain likes or get my followers up in a hurry

But unapologetically and damn justifiably emotional as Carl Thomas in a seemingly drunken demeanor I ask where are all our normally out spoken non colored "friends" at this time that we need them the most

 Or better yet where are the ones that look like us that speak out & post or even regram retweet and openly boast about being so called "woke" and each and everything but what affects us the FUCKING MOST

Confusion and anger tangled rapidly mangles in and then my rant begins

Now my speech becomes slurred with so vivid nearly visible words my mouth wants to say about so many innocent people that look like me dying

Yet it knows not the right position like my eye sights blurred from crying and trying to put the correct sentence together as if the world of my brothers and sister are texting asking me to help with defiance and I'm not replying

And my hands shaking as if I have Parkinson's disease but still not giving a fuck whether it's right or what because the wades in the water we face don't sit well

The current currents of reality create waves of desolation, intimidation and solace

I apologize if this gets you down as I too shed tears as I wrote this

I just couldn't let this pass unnoticed as my day to day routine becomes harder and harder to focus

Unnecessary uncertainty of life security holds notions so cold the polars could not bear them

Faced with minimum outlet to present my vent I turn to you in hopes that the ones you have are better

But truth be told big black and bold a part of me is also hoping that you share them

Whether friends or family I love you all, my people please be careful but never tilt your crowns nor let your light dim

Play With Me

As we toked in what seemed to be steams as strong as engine smoke from river boats like the Delta Queen as they drift down stream

Her head lays in the bed of my chest and she looked directly into my eyes and said to me,

Who the fuck do you think you are?

Really; who are you? And who told you to be so damn great?

I mean if you're this good this early then what/who am I to expect when it gets late?

I'm serious, like really? Like as we grow and go on date after date,

Later on down the line as this relationship forms how will this person I met early on take shape?

No don't you dare smirk like that as if you know something I don't......

"but ohhhohoho just wait"

"Because what I have in store for you will captivate you to the point you hopelessly fall in love with captivation so that you never want to escape"

God dammit see that's what I'm talking about right there

That sunny disposition, that raining/reigning intellect and that intense sense of humor tangled with a mental sexual stare

No no no you won't do this to me have me falling all over the place

Calling me baby I mean literally making me your baby following you crawling all over the place

The Roux Vol. 1

See I've meet you before sir and I will not get got again you know "fool me one once shame on you" ahhhhhh you know the rest

Wait stop..... I know what you're saying lady and I understand your protest

But don't get it twisted now because I've honed these test

And where some have failed horribly and some have excelled the best

As opposed to falling or beating you at this baby I will caress; every inch of your lobe with regal finesse

Rather that beat you I'd rather teach you so eagerly and in turn equally learn from you showing you knowledge holds the most wealth

See you came searching for a mortal sapiosexual yet found God Sapio himself

Now as we both are aware of the cognitive dissonance you parlayed upon with notions of inadequacy

A rebuttal from me would refute the fact that these mind games you chose are far more amusing than the usual fallacies

So I grant you forgiveness in advance as you knew and still know fully not that you bask in the presence of mental royalty

And with that said (well thought actually) before I actually said a word

With a smile adhesively smeared on my face as I softly grab her cheek to pull her closer to me as I gaze into her eyes as if in a daze

facetiously I say

"Hi I'm King, who the fuck are you?"

10
LOVE IN ALL
IT'S MADNESS
BRI GAMBINO

Can I?

I wanna be your person
Your love
Not ya world
Cause there's more to it than just us
I want to put my trust in you and put yours in me
Allow yourself to confide in me
Create plans to live abundantly
Let me hold your secrets
I wanna promise forever with you
But I'm not sure if would you keep it
Are you willing to free up ya heart
Ya soul
Ya mind
I want to help you find peace and love for an unlimited time
Can I nurture your soul

Can I love you till you turn old?

#Together

Looking at you I see something divine
You been showing me things I hadn't seen in a long time
You really amaze me
It sometimes makes me a little crazy
I know I annoy you but that's why I'm baby
Your my light to the dark
My fire spark
The key that unlocks me

When I'm with you I feel alive
I feel anything is achievable
I feel my soul thrive

You speak life into me When I feel like dying
You hold my head high when I'm crying
Help me grow when I feel there's no more growing

But it's still something eating at me that you can't fix
I'm trynna figure out ya ticks, and tricks
Maybe there's not any
But you been acting real distant
A little bit of disinterest
Starting to be inconsistent and malicious

When we go out we everyone's favorite couple
But they don't see our consistent troubles
This faithful struggle

To many things chipping away
Not sure where our relationship will sway
I'm confused
Lost
Not understanding how my best friend, my man
The one who fixed this frown, my crown
Allows me to be clowned, dismissed
Disregarded
Unloved
Maybe I'm the trick

Found My Queen

Looking at you
Seeing something too good to be true
Not knowing how to pin point what it is about you
But my interest you peeked it
Your body language was unique
Some kind of language and no, I cannot speak it
The way you handled me I could not critique
You respected me
You allowed me to be a man
Helped me realize where I stand
That laugh was contagious
And that smile was something outrageous
Your beauty has such a glow
My affection for you I'm ready to show
These steps I'm willing to take
I want your heart and that's something I won't break
Cause with you I've found my queen

11
MUSING
MARISSA FRASER

Musing 1

They make me feel like I'm the black version of the evil queen from the movie, Snow White.
As if I wake up every morning saying, "Mirror, Mirror on the wall...Who's the Baddest Bitch of all??? ....You, Marissa my darling."

Skipping down easy street is what you envision as my life,
But you didn't know me in 2013 when God put me under the knife.
Performing supernatural surgery:
 Beauty for ashes, strength for tears.
... I'd been living in abuse and hatred for too many damn years!!
 You disrespect my beauty and turn it into a joke,
 Have me feeling like a circus clown or a freak at a sideshow.
... But whatever you think this is, it's not a petting zoo so do not touch.
So many times the pressure for perfection can be too much.

If this skin could talk and tell you what it's been through, you wouldn't think the journey to this place in my life was so pretty.
Regeneration of my cells through time,
Magic eraser to my scars,
Transforming my bruises into bronze....
...Or better yet Gold.
 My skin holds stories that have never been told. Or spoken aloud.
My. Skin. Holds. The. Secrets. Of. My. Past.

...Like that time that I had a black eye, and had to lie,
and say, "I was about to open a door when someone on the other side unexpectedly came in...Hitting me on the right side of my face."
...Or that one time that I had a busted lip because my friend slammed so hard on the brakes so hard that I crashed into the dashboard.
...The scratches on my neck came from the neighbor's cat...

....And my nose is bleeding because I just tripped...

When my mom saw the handprints on my arms, I told her that I got cold at night and didn't realize how hard I'd been holding myself.

I never thoughts my first lesson in wearing makeup would come from man...
Who would teach me to understand the right color concealer to make his sins look crystal clean.
 Maybe she's being abused, or maybe it's Maybelline?
Put makeup on my memories....
Until His hand came down and healed me!
Shed the old and rebirthed me!
 Destroying the evidence of when he hurt me!!

So when I hear that you think I'm a narcissist,
I just remember that I'm blessed.
Ignore when you cut me down and try to make me feel like I'm less.
 It's funny how you think the words you say have got me stressed....
Because I'm proud when I look in the mirror and know I survived another trial and test.

Musing 2

I'm tired of feeling like I'm not good enough.
I've been trying to write more poems, but I keep getting stuck.
Insecurity adds pounds to my pen until I can't bear the weight any longer.
I crumble under pressure.
I crumble up another page of this notebook.
Another potential masterpiece.
I have....no peace of mind....when I realize that my wastebasket is overflowing with dreams that are so easy for me to throw away.
All because. I'm too afraid. To say what I want to say....
Feel like I'm not worthy to even touch the mic on this stage.
When I reality, my gut is in a rage....
From the words that burn on my heart that I choose to swallow.
I take this gift for granted and assume I'll be promised tomorrow.
God has spoiled me
Beyond measure or belief, I should be dead.
Been given so many chances, I should be grateful for the opportunity to speak every word that comes into my head.
Yet I continue to hold my breath.
Pretend like writer's block is what's blocking me,
When I'm the only one who's stopping me. Self-sabotage.
I struggle to throw my thoughts together. Collage.
The vision of me being a successful writer is starting to look like a mirage.
Now you see it.
Now you don't.
I choke on stale sentences that I allow to rot at the back of my throat.

I'm tired of feeling like I'm not good enough.
Constantly comparing myself to everyone else when I'm my own biggest enemy.
Possess the power of the spirit, but you'll never hear it.
My lips produce spoiled fruit...
From the seeds I plant in my head. I steady neglect, they end up dead.

In case you're wondering why my eyes are always red,
I'm mourning.....
my lost....
train....
of thought.
I treat every poems that never existed like my miscarried children.

Moment of silence.

If silence is do golden, then why is it the one thing that's killing me softly...
From the inside out.
I die a little but more every time I keep my words inside of my mouth.
I'm not proud
Of being too much of a Coward to speak out. Spit it out!
Call me poetic masochist,
I bring this upon myself.
I put all of my aspirations behind everyone else,
Collecting dust on my mental shelf. I need help.

I have poetic Blue Balls and I ready to Bust!
From so much built up frustration,
I feel like I'm on the cusp...
Of Greatness.
Please forgive me for my lateness.
I'm ready to shake off self-hatred.

This poem is my confession.
Pressure lifting off of my chest.

It's finally my turn to Exhale.

Musing 3

The other day someone told me that they had never been attracted to a black girl until they met me.

Was that supposed to be a compliment???

All I want to ask is, WHY!!!

Don't you see that your twisted view of beauty is what makes my Sisters run home and cry??

But the thing is that you'll never see those tears on our faces....

They're manifested in the clench of a Jaw.

The strength in our stride.

Refusing to let oppression strip us of our pride.

Because If you haven't noticed, there's only one thing us black women are lacking and that would be the respect we're owed.

Treated like Bronze, when really we're Gold.

Formed in the image of perfection. Big nose, Big lips, Big hair, BIG heart.

And if you can't handle that, I feel sorry for you because you're missing out on appreciating the true essence of art.

We love with a passion as strong as Samson, like an all-consuming fire.

So much that we supply but it's hard to find a buyer..

When ignorance and prejudice is so prevalent, all there's left to develop is independence.

...And what's sexier than that?

Our will is as powerful and unmoved as our naps.

Tired of hearing men devalue us and proclaim to only prefer a certain race.

My fist clenched and I bite my lip as I think to myself, "Nigga don't make me put you in your place!"

When God created us, he did so without blemish or flaw.

Not just for black girls but for the colors of all.

I love the skin I'm in, and I would never change it.

Ignore anyone who thinks differently,

They're just mad because they're basic.

12

PIECES TO THE PUZZLE

CHARNICA JORDACHEA

Together

I don't know you well, but i love you
As crazy as that sounds
& I wish that things could be different

If it weren't for life's bounds.
I wish we could have been.. Together.
You see we each hold free will
But as a child- your parents decide for you
& ours decided early on that growing up was something we wouldn't do.. Together
It hurt being separated
I didn't get to watch you grow year over year
& when you had tough days- I wasn't there to wipe away tears
When you had your first crush, I wasn't there to tease
At the lowest of times- I wish I was there to pray with you- hands folded, on our Knees... together
I understood what it meant to be a family

Since like clockwork, after school I watched family matters & the Cosby Show
But that temporary relief stung like a bee when the tv went off because i had no there
With me.
At least with each of you, individually, I did see seasons

& I won't count them any less than they are
It's just when you're forced to make up for lost time just to be separated again.. It Makes life even more hard.

It was like scolding hot food touched my tongue.

I was mute- knowing I had my own but unable to experience those intimate feelings

I sat- like a stop sign just watching others laugh, cry & stick up for one another.
I was a jealous mess
I tried "substituting" family into my life to fill the void in my heart

It made things worse because none of them stuck around so I became paranoid
& I accepted we'd never be together
Years have passed & I'm now an adult
I've tried to put the past behind me because i no longer wanted to live with bruises on
My heart.

But the truth is I'm so afraid of having a family of my own. I never want my children to
Experience life growing up without being together.

Charnica Jordachea

You Don't Own Me

You don't own me.

I may come in with a smile
On my face

I may control my style
To fit the dress code for your workplace
I may keep my hair straight

& speak an octave higher than i actually do
Because that's what you claim makes the money for you
But you don't own me
You have made sly comments & i've turned the other cheek

I've ignored the the disrespect & kept my attitude meek
No longer able to perform my best when everything i do is critiqued
Carrying the weight of wanting to speak up without looking weak
But you don't own me
It doesn't matter that i've given my time, energy & sometimes my soul
It didn't matter that you set, i met & even surpassed the damn goal
Hell because i am a black woman working in the corporate industry
Meaning it was an extreme reach in thinking there would be real loyalty... for me??
Ha! But you don't own me...
& there's no such thing as job security
Least that's what you were sure to keep reminding me
I was forced out of a place that i once felt safe in
Called folks family- i was sadly mistaken
Now after being released from the chains that had me bound & locked away
I wake up with a grateful heart ready to take on the day

That chapter of my life is closed- sigh- but i cannot walk away & say i didn't learn many
Life lessons
I'll forever be tougher than most & that was a blessing hidden in the stressing.

You don't own me..
I'm free!

Charnica Jordachea

A Daughter Scorned

Somebody rockin knockin da boots..
That's the only young childhood memory i have of you
& that was when I was like
...two?
4 children you bore & you didn't raise any of us
It's no wonder why it's hard for me to trust
You missed so much....
But I'm good though.
Gratefully Sex Ed started in elementary school
So I knew exactly what to do when my period began at 14..
I didn't need you
I remember when mother's day would roll in and
I'd make cards for my father or whoever was in charge of the house where I was
..living
Then I started filling in
& I had the juice that all the boys wanted to sip &
My own daddy even began to start looking..
At me, passing blunts & touching me until he finally inserted himself in me..
.. Where were you then mom?!
Living your best life, huh
I fended for myself
Spoke up for myself.
& was sent to you as a punishment
So he wouldn't have a case and go to jail.
Meeting you
As I was coming to live with you
As a teenager who grew up knowing she wasn't good enough..
It was tragic
Despite that- I was like a newborn & yearned for my mother's love.
I was willing to forgive & forget but you- you didn't want to be a mother
You.. Wanted an associate,
An equal.. &
Even then you grew tired of me for standing up for you
You & your choice of trash ass men.
So you sent me to live with your friend..

Holidays were the worst days
Was burden to families making sure I didn't feel left out on Christmas & my birthday.
Still get teary eyes for every gift I receive to this day.
Painful ass memories
But god had different plans for me
He sent a mentor in my direction
She told me if I wanted preservation
Over my life I needed to make my own lane
Do my own thing
Told me I had the power to change the game
So I got my shit together
Made the decision that I wanted to be better
Instead of another version of you
Had to force myself to believe that what I had accepted as life before wasn't true & it
Wouldn't do.
I went on & graduated from college, started a career, & even got married without you
& all to see you now on social media trying to take credit??
I'll give you credit
So "mom".. Thank you
For showing me what type of mother I don't want to be
When I become a mother
My daughter will know what she looked like as a baby.
She'll know her family tree,
Her history..
& not just what you can find on Facebook.
I'll be at every parent teacher conference & every class presentation or spelling bee.
She will lack no support from me.
She will always have someone cheering her on at every step show
& I'll be at every concert to hear her sing.
I won't dare to miss her senior prom.
She'll be able to purchase her year book & her class ring.
I'll do my best to lead by example and I'll be sure to pray
I vow to support my children's growth & future every day, in every way
It's a big responsibility to be a parent I know this much is true
But you shouldn't have kids if being a mother is too much for you
But amen

Because through it all I've learned how to blossom despite my wilted roots..
& ironically my favorite song of all time is still "knockin da boots"

Charnica Jordachea

13

A NEW CONCEPT FOR A BEGINNING MAN

KENNETH SANDERS III

A Letter From A King

My anger did nothing for me
But invited me into a place they wanted me to stay
Trying to build more rage inside of me.
Instead I release my anxieties through these pages
Hoping to be a man of clear consciousness and thinking
Pain residing within every step I take to look for love
But still yet I guess nobody want to see nothing but the thug
People take my lessons and confuse it to being their blessings
You forget I'm the one on the inside looking out so
I see changes before they occur
A proud king but being prideful is something that I have to block out. Because someday soon my queen will come
And she will be my match made from heaven
So I'm going to cherish every moment spent amongst her
Never rushing what we build
Understanding each other's past makes our future that much brighter!
So when you see us throw roses down so we can walk on them
Know it's because you are in the presence of our kingdom.

Regression

Benefits that comes from not allowing power to be transfer into the next
                person.
Keeping a clear head because you tighten your own reins when anger
                conquer your situation.
Never doubting the positive flow of energy endowed through your creation
                for life.
Destruction lives in a dark place, turn from it and advance to the true light. For what they see on the surface makes them misunderstand the potential
                of its nature.
Believing in myself, I acknowledge the hardships I will encounter on my
                pursuit for patience.

Music to the Divine

Divine aspiration, persistence through confrontation
Injustice for shortcomings of the next man's falling
Adapting to situations upon nature change
Because of the refusal to failure toward one's name
Depending on the wisdom of a woman allows a man to bathe in the
        essence of serenity.
Calling her name while sleep
Hoping for an answer and her appearance of first sight!
Does she believe a man can become so embedded with her presence
        that he cultivates a strength to knock all barriers down?
The being of two currents in an ocean creates a whirlpool intertwining the
        meaning of how opposites attracts.

ABOUT THE AUTHORS

Candy Weeks

Hey everyone Candy here! I'm stepping out of my box somewhat by sharing my writing with you. I've been writing poetry since the late 90's. It was then discovered my best friend wrote poetry beautifully so I decided to try my hand at it. From that moment it became a cathartic way of relieving what was on my heart and mind. At the time keeping a diary seemed like asking to have my privacy invaded, so I didn't. Being already in love with words and their meaning I thought of poetry as a way to code my thoughts and feelings. This will be the first time but not the last for my passion to be published. Hope you enjoy!

Kenya Turner Washington

Kenya Turner Washington is a Licensed Clinical Social Worker, Mental Health Therapist, Speaker, Poet and Reiki Healer. Kenya is married with two children, Kenya earned her MSW from the University of Oklahoma. She has worked with women, men, children and families of all ages and backgrounds. One of her missions in life is to help others recognize who they are and the gifts they have. To not let past hurts and mistakes hinder you. Scars are just a testimony that you made it through. You may be going through something in your life, it's just a chapter in your book not the whole story

Kenneth Sanders

Kenneth Sanders III I was born on March 6, 1989 in Wichita, Kansas but raised in Tulsa, Oklahoma. Honestly music had always been a favorite of his but since he come to learn poetry, he has gained a more profound appreciation going into a relationship, friendship or just being amongst family. He has made mistakes just as well as the next person but what he has gotten out of it turned into joy and blessings for him. Currently, he's on a soul-searching journey and trying to build his future a little more every day. He attended Marion Anderson and Andrew Jackson Elementary, he went through Hamilton Middle School and attended a few high schools but he obtained his GED.

Karmen S. Williams

Karmen S. Williams is a California native and raised in Oklahoma. She has lived and traveled to various lands experiencing and learning from cultures. Karmen being a true introvert, has been writing thoughts, poetry, plays, and stories since she learned to write. She received her doctorate in 2016 and is currently a public health and health services researcher. Karmen is naturally optimistic and uses this art form to convey hope and vision of great possibilities to the human race.

Demeatrice Hall

Demeatrice L. Hall (De) is a native of Tulsa, Oklahoma. A graduate of Raymond S. McLain High School. As well as a Mother of three.
De loves to write poetry. Often using it as a way to express as well as free herself from daily experiences. De is a Healthcare Administration and Business Computer Technology Graduate moving toward Entrepreneurship.

Connie Turner

Connie Turner, was born and raised in Oakland, California. She loved reading romance magazines just to loose herself in a fantasy at an early age. She is a mother of 3. After divorcing for the 3rd time she moved to Oklahoma and is in a wonderful relationship. She started writing poetry and found that her erotic poems were big hits with friends. Although she does write other genres that she is passionate about, eroticism seems to be her niche. She is member of a poetry group on Facebook, "Taste of Poetry Flow " This is her first attempt at publishing any of her work, Enjoy!

Webster L. Wortham

Webster Wortham is a Tulsa native. Born and raised in North Tulsa, this McClain Scot has given back to his community in various capacities. Serving on the McClain Foundation Board and as career advisor with Tulsa tech, Webster provides immediate opportunities for success to Students in underserved neighborhoods. His past volunteer activities include serving as a Big Brother with Big Brothers and Big Sisters of Oklahoma, J Parle' Scholarship Fund, Habitat for Humanity, and occasional honey do with the ladies of Alpha Chi Omega Chapter. When he's not working or volunteering he enjoys making music, and spending time with his wife Jerica and their sons Solomon and Jonah.

Marissa Fraser

Marissa is a 26 year-old creative who lives in Tulsa, OK, but has strong Jamaican roots. She has been writing since grade school, but officially started performing spoken word poetry in 2014. Most of her work is inspired by real-life experiences.

Tosha Craft

Tosha Craft is a poet, writer, speaker, and educator who doesn't mind laying it all on the line as long it helps someone else. She has spent most of her years mentoring and inspiring others to push past their obstacles and be better. Teaching is her passion. Her primary purpose in life is to educate and empower in all she does by engaging people of diverse backgrounds, cultures and denominations. With her passionate personality, Tosha captivates her audiences by drawing them in with a personal, down-home approach. She is open and receptive, candid and compassionate, only asking for the listener to be open to the exchange.

A graduate of Northeastern State University with a B.A. in English, she went on to attain her M.Ed. at Langston University. Fully committed to the cause of motivating others and being active in her community, she spends her days teaching teens to read, write, and speak their truth. She lives hers every time she graces a stage. Her poetry and prose has been featured in J'Parle Literary magazine with live performances at the Living Arts of Tulsa and J'Parle Live. She is currently penning *Love, Sex and other Addictions*, a poetry book dedicated to the taboo. Follow Tosha Craft on Twitter @tosha_craft and Instagram @toshacraft.

Bri Gambino

Bri Gambino is a young entrepreneur who originated from Chicago but has spent most of her adult life in Tulsa, Ok . She is a model, poet, and an artist. She is the creator of Plush LLC, which empowers women to love who they are and what they got. She has been in fashion shows, music videos, and is creating movie scripts. At a young age, poetry became the best way for her to voice her feelings when she felt she couldn't be heard. Her understanding of the lessons that life has taught her is what inspires her poems

Charnica Jordachea

Charnica (Bridges) Bullock is from South Carolina & moved to Oklahoma in December 2016. Her career has been in Property Management for the last 9 years but she is now taking on full-time entrepreneurship. She is married to her college sweetheart, Cyrus Bullock & writes poetry as therapy. This is her first time having any of her work published.

Jerica D. Wortham Visionary Author

Jerica D. Wortham is a Tulsa, OK native with an international spirit. Jerica has been writing, and performing her poetry since the tender age of 11. In May 2012 Jerica founded J PARLE' LLC, and started J PARLE' Literary Magazine. This endeavor gathered artists from all around the country, and provided a platform to those that were in some instances more comfortable with the pen than the mic.... The mission: to give every voice a chance to be heard. In 2013 she was presented with the opportunity to host her very first live show; and J PARLE' Live was born! An author, business coach, and philanthropist, in October 2014 she founded the J Parle' Scholarship fund where she was able to award local students and adults with money to continue or pursue their education. In 2018 she founded J Parle' Publishing helping artist to realize their dreams of being published. When she is not working she enjoys spending time with her husband Webster, and their two sons Solomon and Jonah.

If you're interested in being on her mailing lists email JPARLELLC@ymail.com.

You can also stay up to date through Facebook.com/JPARLELLC

www.ingramcontent.com/pod-product-compliance
Lightning Source LLC
Chambersburg PA
CBHW070307100426
42743CB00011B/2379